Class No.

Book Order Details

Order No: 936429

Date: JuLY 4 '23 ✓ Rev

Supplier: Browns

Cost: £8.99

Barcode No: R70840

Class No: 158.1

The world's speeded up. Bad stuff like stress, anxiety, depression and burnout are on the rise. Meantime, the world's reserves of happiness are at an all-time low.

But just because the world's gone mad, it doesn't mean you have to.

'Brilliant Schools' provides training and resources aimed at equipping children and young people with knowledge and skills so they can take charge of their own mental health. We're part of the world famous 'Art of Being Brilliant'. We specialise in positive psychology and mental WEALTH. Basically, it's science, heavily disguised as rollicking good fun.

Check us out at
www.artofbrilliance.co.uk &
www.brilliant.school

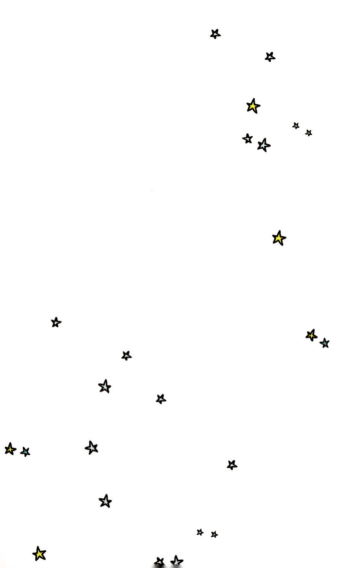

A Brillant Life

A 'Brilliant Schools' Book

brought to life by Amy

There was once a young person who got by in life.

Raj

James

Conner

Oscar

or **Something.**

His name was James or Oscar or Raj or Connor. Or whoever.

He was age 8 or 16 or 11 or 14. Or something.

Everything was just kinda OK.

You know, average.

He did alright at school. But he was a young person and everyone knows that kids moan. James or Oscar or Raj or Connor (or whoever), had an A✭ in grumbling. And he had a point, right? Life's so unfair, what with homework, coursework, school and exams. And everyone struggles to get out of bed, don't they?

Like most young people, his negativity had started to become a habit.

One day he was daydreaming in maths and accidentally worked out that the average lifespan is 4000 weeks. That's quite a lot, but not enough weeks to waste being average.

It was a wakey-wakey moment. James or Oscar or Raj or Connor (or whoever) decided to change. He learned some stuff - and became brilliant.

This is what he learned. His **'Big 5'** were life-changing.

Oh, and he didn't just learn the **Big 5...**

...he actually did them. Wow!

First, he chose his attitude.

Positive

NEGATIVE

He actually decided to be positive.

Which was very difficult when those around him weren't. Especially in the boring lessons (and there were lots of those). Everybody else continued to moan that life wasn't fair. But James or Oscar or Raj or Connor (or whoever) decided school was an opportunity to get on in life. He would tackle it with a 'can do' attitude.

Next (and this was a bit spooky) he learned that when he chose to be positive, nice things happened to him. Things seemed to turn out a whole lot better. The world was great. Lessons were easier. Maths could be fun.

IMAGINE!

And when he was positive he smiled more. It was kinda weird, but his positivity seemed to leak out of him so those around him felt amazing too.

He'd stumbled on the second of the 'Big 5' He realised he was having a huge impact on those around him - much bigger than he'd ever imagined. In fact, he twigged it was bigger than that. He realised that he could not NOT have an impact. His attitude leaked whether he wanted it to or not.

James or Oscar or Raj or Connor (or whoever) realised his emotions were infectious. He had a super-power! He was

Impact Man.

Now which impact should I choose? Positive or negative? Mmmm, tricky one, eh?

Our hero chose well. He realised it was the most powerful choice in the world. (He did wonder why nobody else seemed to be making the right choice, but he didn't let others' negative attitudes stop him from feeling brilliant).

With a can-do attitude and positive impact in the bag, he decided he wanted his life to GO LARGE. James or Oscar or Raj or Connor (or whoever) started to set himself some huge goals

Really big ones that were scary at first. So he broke them down into little steps and started to make them happen. Strangely enough, a lot of his huge goals were dependent on how much effort he put into his school work. And, of course, with his positive attitude already in the bag, he made big progress. Very quickly.

And he **NEVER** gave up on his goals - even when things got tough. Which was often. The next thing he learned was a real bummer. Those people who grumbled about life 'not being fair' - they were right! He discovered that even when he did his level best to be brilliant, things still went wrong.

Maths was sometimes really hard.

Like SERIOUSLY rock hard.

It actually did rain a lot. Even on Saturdays.

And homework/tests/exams just kept on coming.

Then, **Ping!**

James or Oscar or Raj or Connor (or whoever) had one of those penny dropping moments. It's true that life isn't fair, but who said it was supposed to be fair in the first place?

NOBODY. That's who!

Nobody in the history of the world had actually decreed that life was supposed to be fair.

So when a bad day came, he took it on the chin. It was perfectly okay to not be okay.

But James or Oscar or Raj or Connor (or whoever) didn't have many 'not okay' days because he'd learned the fourth point of the

'Big 5'.

He had BOUNCEBACKABILITY.

He kept coming back to the 4000 weeks thing. It focused his mind on how valuable time was. He decided life was too short to waste being anything less than his best self.

When he caught himself being negative he thought about his 4000 weeks and quickly bungeed back to being positive. He learned to ask himself a very simple question:

How would the best version of me react?

He practised until this became his normal way of thinking and behaving (he learned that practise makes PERMANENT).

He now had 4 of the **'Big 5'**. He had chosen to be positive, he understood the massive impact he was having on those around him, he set huge goals and had some bouncebackability.

Positive

But the last one was a **biggy**. Like proper massive.

He realised he had to take responsibility for his future. For young people, this was the hardest thing to do.

rubbish school

rubbish clothes

rubbish smartphone

He noticed others blaming their rubbish life on their teachers, relationships and the fact that they didn't have the latest designer clothes or the smartest smartphone. Some actually blamed their mood on Mondays.

rubb
te

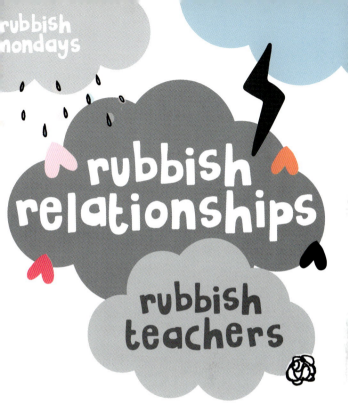

rubbish mondays

rubbish relationships

rubbish teachers

In fact, the more he listened, the more he heard teenagers blaming everyone but themselves. 'My teacher's rubbish.' 'I've got too much homework.' 'My mum nags me.' 'Science is so boring.'

rubbish homework

James or Oscar or Raj or Connor (or whoever) noticed it was always someone else's fault.

He smiled. He knew happiness wasn't really about designer clothes. He'd probably never have an actual bang-up-to-date phone. And a 7th of his entire life was gonna be lived on Mondays. That was a big chunk of time. Too much to waste!

He knew that happiness was about the choices he made and the positive attitude he carried with him.

James or Oscar or Raj or Connor (or whoever) had taken personal responsibility for changing himself. He quit blaming others. Or circumstances. Or the drizzle. Or double Maths on a Monday morning. He realised he could take charge of his life.

old me

the
NEW
me

James or Oscar or Raj or Connor (or whoever) wanted results, not excuses. So he made a massive breakthrough. He stopped thinking about the **'Big 5'** and started doing them instead.

At first it was difficult coz the energy vampires were everywhere. They were really good at being negative. In fact, they were better than good, they were experts!

The energy vampires were brilliant at sucking the happiness out of every person and every situation. **They had a POINT.**

The weather is always rubbish, isn't it? And the school bus is always late. And then there's 'Scary McLary' his maths teacher. Oh, and homework.

Scary!

But James or Oscar or Raj or Connor (or whoever) practised being positive, even when surrounded by the energy vampires. (He was a brave young man).

ZooOom

He noticed the sun shone loads. And the bus was often on time. And if he knuckled down Mrs Mclary was ace. In fact, she was proper helpful and smiley. Who knew! As for homework, it still needed doing but he took pride in doing it better than he had to.

He tried ever so hard, he was even happy when it rained. I mean, why be upset about the weather? And the more he tried, the easier it became.

Smiley Clary

It wasn't long before James or Oscar or Raj or Connor (or whoever's) life changed for the better. He actually wanted to get out of bed. After all, he had goals to achieve.

Very quickly, he became brilliant. Other people noticed his cheery smile and positive outlook.

Teachers noticed.

His **parents** noticed. His **mates** noticed.

But **HE** noticed the most.

His gran was super-proud.

And just in case you were wondering how it all turned out, James or Oscar or Raj or Connor (or whoever) got some stellar grades and a worthwhile career. He lived to a ripe old age (way beyond 4000 weeks).

He smiled a lot. His wrinkles were happy.

And he inspired lots of people, especially his children.

Who turned out brilliant too.

The END.

NOW
for some
serious
thinking:

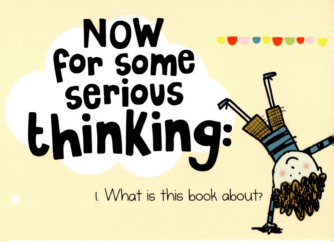

1. What is this book about?

....
....

2. WHO is this book really about?

....
....

3. What have you learned?

....
....

4. How can you apply the learning to **YOUR** life?

5. What would be the result if you did?

6. What would be the result if you didn't?

7. What's stopping **YOU**?

8. What 3 things do you need to **START** doing (or do more of) that will help you achieve?

....

....

....

9. What 3 things do you need to **STOP** doing (or do less of) that will help you achieve?

....

....

....

10. Who are you at your best?

....

....

....

....

11. Think back to the last time you felt amazing.
    List 6 words that describe you at your best.

12. Imagine the best version of you.
    Describe that person.
    What is their motto in life?

13. If someone was making a speech about you,
    what would you like them to say?

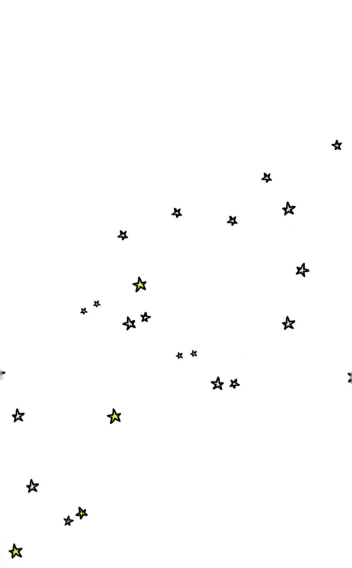

STOP READING, FLIP the BOOK,

because learning never ends

STOP READING,
FLIP THE
BOOK

because learning never ends

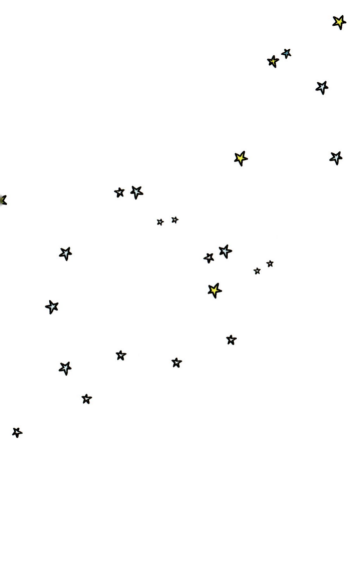

7. Imagine you are 30 years old & life has been great. Complete the following sentence in less than 30 words: **I've achieved some great things because...**

8. Most of us have been touched deeply by a few important people. People who, because of their feelings for us have helped us become who we are today. Some of what these people gave to us was uplifting and inspiring. Sometimes, we didn't really appreciate them, until now! Maybe they worked during the day and looked after the household too. Maybe they gave us time. They helped us get through difficult times, or offered good advice. Maybe it's a teacher, or parent, or grandparent, or a friend?

Write a letter to this person. Tell the person what he or she has done for you, the impact they've had and how grateful you are. Tell them what you've learned from them. Write from your heart.

9. Send it.

4. What's the key to your successful future?

5. What 3 things will you **DO** to load life in your favour?

6. What 3 things will you **stop** doing to improve your lot?

2. Imagine you are an alien visting planet earth. Your mission is to find the secret of 'happiness' and take it back to your planet. What 'secret' would you take back?

3. Run 2 movies in your head:

Movie 1 is a black & white film of the 'average' you. Close your eyes and picture your future. What job and relationship do you have? Where does your average you live? How much does the average you smile?

Movie 2 is the full colour 3D 'extraordinary' you. Go on, run the movie!
Check out your future now. You'll see a definite increase in the smile rate!

Thinking time...

Rhianna's story is based on research into happiness and positivity. To cut an incredibly long story short, you can learn to become positive. And having a positive, confident and upbeat approach to life will get you better results at home, at work, on holiday and even in the supermarket.

The problem is, it's a lot easier to be negative! People can get stuck in whinge mode. I've met some who've become experts at it, honing their negative powers for 50 years or more!

The great news is that the earlier you get into positive habits the better it is for you and all those around you. So here are a few things to think about:

1. What's the **key** to Rhianna's success?

teeth nearly came out. The room filled with laughter and applause.

'Quiet please,' I have a few words to say about the birthday girl,' announced Danny.

He stood by his wife and held her hand. His thumb rubbed her wrinkles and then squeezed tight. He smiled at his beautiful wife. She beamed back. Rhianna's mind went back to her decision 86 years ago.

An extraordinary decision, she thought.

And an extraordinary life.

The END.

Rhianna sat down, exhausted. All that dancing had worn her out. But, hey, it's good to dance at your 100th birthday bash.

Rhianna looked around at the smiling faces. Her eyes sparkled. Her laughter lines were deep. She was surrounded by family and friends.

It's been an extraordinary journey.

The band started playing and everyone sang 'Happy Birthday'.

Rhianna felt tears welling but now wasn't the time.

She blew out the 100 candles and her false

Mr Baker shouted less. At least at her.

And if there was an Olympics for moaning, Rhianna realised a lot of her mates would be going for gold.

But not our Rhianna. The 90/10 game of life meant she couldn't control the homework. It was coming whether she liked it or not. So she decided to welcome it. She attacked her homework like she devoured her lessons, with energy and enthusiasm.

Done!

Sometimes she even handed her homework in early. And it was superb.

Rhianna felt proud.

The 90% was much more interesting. Rhianna figured that 90% of whether she had a good day or bad day was down to how she reacted to the 10%.

So when she lined up to go into French she thought, 'I can't control the lesson, but I can choose how I respond to the lesson.' And silly as it may seem, she began to feel positive about it. Plus, it was only an hour and everyone can try their hardest for an hour.

So she did.

And when the weather was rubbish (like nearly every day) and everyone else was whinging, Rhianna applied the 90/10 principle. 'I can't control the weather,' she told herself, 'but I absolutely can choose to be positive about it. I mean, some people live in the desert and would dance with joy if it rained this hard.'

And then there was homework.

Oh boy, there was plenty of homework!

Of course, being positive didn't mean that rubbish things stopped happening. That would be ridiculous. It still rained, for example. And she still had to go to French (which she still didn't particularly like)

But she invented a game that she played in her head. Rhianna called it the 90/10 game.

Rhianna figured that 90/10 was actually a game of life and it goes like this...

10% of whether Rhianna had a good or bad day was down to circumstances. This 10% consisted of stuff that Rhianna couldn't control. Like French, or the drizzle, or homework. Or Mr Baker shouting at her in science.

She figured that these things were going to happen to her anyway.

She had a word for these things:

'Life'

Rhianna practised being her best self until it became normal. In fact, after a few weeks, people started expecting her to be bright, cheery, enthusiastic and hard working.

She felt great and, guess what, so did the people around her.

Average

She wondered why she'd spent fourteen years being average. What a waste!

Still, the past was in the past. It was the bright future that counted.

For the right reasons.

Her teachers were commenting. Her Gran was super-proud. Her mum was delighted.

Even Danny had noticed her!

Yikes!

Rhianna's positive approach meant she smiled more. Spooky stuff was happening. She noticed three massive things:

Firstly, school was fun and kind of easier. She couldn't quite put her finger on it but she imagined it must be something to do with the fact that when she did her very best, she accidentally learned loads more.

In a spooky twist of the universe, the teachers became super-helpful.

Second, even 'Terrible Tuesday' was cool. Oh my gosh! Rhianna twigged that it wasn't the subjects that had been getting her down. It was the way she'd been *thinking* about them.

So all she really had to do was re-think her thinking.

And third, people liked her more. It was like a super-power. It's not as though Rhianna had been short of friends, but the extraordinary version of her was getting noticed.

Her life improved.

In fact her life improved very quickly. She'd raised her game. For fourteen years Rhianna had got out of bed because she had to. Her mum sometimes had to shout upstairs a dozen times or more.

Not anymore.

Because now Rhianna had decided to get out of bed because she *wanted* to.

'Rise and whine' had been replaced by 'rise and SHINE'.

And because she'd decided to be extraordinary, she no longer stomped downstairs like a tousle-haired grump monster. Rhianna was a pleasure to have at the brekky table.

Homework... better than I have to. Tick.

Attitude... more positive than I have to. Tick.

Manners... more polite than I have to. Tick.

Effort... try harder than I have to. Tick.

Exercise... a bit more than I have to. Tick.

Health eating... a bit more fruit and veg than I have to. Tick.

As her tick-list got ticked, she felt amaaaaaZing.

Rhianna's extraordinary decision to upgrade her attitude meant she sprang out of bed with more energy. She had purpose.

Her aim was to enjoy the day. Imagine? Setting out to actually *enjoy* every day. Even Mondays?

She started to do things better than she had to.

'I think Rhianna's been abducted and replaced by an alien. A hard working, friendly one. Most probably from a galaxy far, far away.'

Thanks
Mr J!

On the way out she thanked Mr Jenkins for a great lesson. 'And I'll be doing the best homework I can,' she grinned. Naturally, Mr Jenkins nearly fainted. He hot-footed it to the staffroom to spread the news.

She knew that Mr J was giving homework so she'd learn stuff that would help her get stellar grades. And great grades were key to 'Extraordinary Rhianna's' next seventy years. She'd run the movie in her head.

She wanted **THAT** future.
A blockbuster future.

Wahoooooo

This future was so amazing that her decision was made, right there and then. She was going to be her best self. It was what Rhianna called a 'no-brainer'.

She wanted results, not excuses.

And guess what, she only went and did it. Rhianna upgraded.

She changed.

She stopped trying to be like everyone else and started to be herself, *brilliantly*.

Mr Jenkins noticed first. He handed out some maths homework and, predictably, the class groaned. Jamie rolled his eyes. Sasha said it wasn't fair. Bekki explained to Sir that she couldn't do it because she had stacks of other homework piled up.

But Rhianna didn't groan. Sure, it was tempting but she smiled instead.

It didn't matter what anyone else was doing. It mattered what *she* was doing.

Rhianna pondered. Sure, she'd have to make some changes. She used her imagination. What would 'Extraordinary Rhianna' look like? And what would she sound like? What kind of attitude would she have? How would it feel to be her best self - on a regular basis?

Rhianna wasn't quite convinced so she closed her eyes and ran two movies in her head. Movie one was a bit bleak. She imagined 'average Rhianna' and life seemed dreary. It was a black and white movie with not much happening. In fact, boy, was it dull.

She ran movie two in her head. Gosh! This was full colour 3-D 'Extraordinary Rhianna', a blockbuster of a life full of thrills, excitement, happiness, a great career, wonderful relationships and bags of fun.

Rhianna had brilliant days. In fact she had a special name for them. She called them 'Saturdays'.

She had okay days too. But some were just rubbish, like 'Terrible Tuesdays' for example, when she had double maths, French and PE.

Nightmare!

Then one day, out of the blue, Rhianna did some thinking. Some *serious* thinking...

She thought about her life. She'd used up 14 years and figured that if she looked after herself, she could expect another 70. Maybe?

Her thought was this: maybe I should aim higher than 'fine'?

What if I started being 'extraordinary Rhianna'? A Rhianna that made other people go 'WOW!'

And what if I started **NOW**?
Wow! Now? But how?

She tended not to rise and shine. For Rhianna it was more like 'rise and whine'.

Nooooooo!

Rhianna was fine.

Well, as fine as any other young person. School was okay. It was a bit of a drag to be honest. You know, what with all that learning, homework, tests, relationships and stuff.

The Game of Life

A 'Brilliant Schools' Book

brought to life by Amy

The world's speeded up. Bad stuff like stress, anxiety, depression and burnout are on the rise. It sometimes feels as though happiness is hanging on in there by it's fingertips.

Just because the world's gone mad, it doesn't mean you have to.

'Brilliant Schools' provides training and resources aimed at equipping children and young people to be able to take charge of their own mental health.

We're part of the world famous 'Art of Being Brilliant'. We specialise in positive psychology and mental WEALTH. Basically, it's science, heavily disguised as rollicking good fun

Check us out at
www.artofbrilliance.co.uk
& www.brilliant.school